WILDLIFE WORLDS

AFRICA

Tim Harris

W
FRANKLIN WATTS
LONDON·SYDNEY

Franklin Watts
First published in Great Britain in 2019 by The Watts Publishing Group

HB ISBN: 978 1 4451 6685 8
PB ISBN: 978 1 4451 6686 5

Printed in Dubai

Series Editor: Amy Pimperton
Series Designer: Nic Davies smartdesignstudio.co.uk
Picture researchers: Rachelle Morris (Nature Picture Library),
Laura Sutherland (Nature Picture Library), Diana Morris

Picture credits:
Alamy: Blickwinkel 2t, 28; Eric Nathan 6-7.
Nature PL: Eric Baccega 23bl; Jim Clare 21cr; Christophe Courteau 2b, 10-11; John Downer 12-13c; Nick Garbutt 14c, 15bl, 19tl; Edwin Giesbers 15br; Tony Heard 10bl; Klien & Hubert 15t; Denis Huot 17l, 20, 31t; Jabruson 22t, 22bl; Roy Mangersnes 13tr, 30t; Juan Carlos Muñoz front cover b, 9b; Inaki Relazon 29c; Anup Shah: 17br; Enrique Lopez-Tapia 9tr; Kim Taylor 11br; Staffen Widstrand 18-19c.
Shutterstock: African Wildcat 6bl; Andrew Allport 7tr; Alslutsky 23br; AndreaAnita back cover tcl, 1t, 5br, 19tr; Selim B 27tl; Stefano Barzellott 14bl; Radek Borovka 8c; Richard Boycott 7bl; Seyms Brugger front cover t, 3br, 19br; Volodymyr Burdiak 16; davemhuntphotography 25tl; Jon Duncan back cover tl, 3tr, 24; Evenfh 11tl; Michael Fitzsimmons 5tr, 25tr; Peter Fodor back cover tr; Mike Gatt back cover tcr, 21br; Homo Cosmicos 4-5bg, 26-27c; Anton Ivanov 11bl, 32t; Andrea Izzotti 9tl; Tomas Kotouc 8bl; Serguei Koultchitskii 21l; Andrzej Kubik 4br, 17tr; Ivan Marjanovic 3cr, 29t; Martin Mecnarowski 27br; Anna Om 17cr, 30t; Angela N Perryman 7br; Patrick Poendl 26bl; Ondrej Prosicky 23tr; Cheryl Ramalho 4cr, 32br; Reptiles4all 27bl; Thomas Retterath 13tl; Jane Rix 25b.

Franklin Watts
An imprint of
Hachette Children's Group
Part of The Watts Publishing Group
Carmelite House
50 Victoria Embankment
London EC4Y 0DZ
An Hachette UK Company

www.hachette.co.uk
www.franklinwatts.co.uk

With thanks to the Nature Picture Library

Contents

African Continent

Africa is the second-largest continent. It is almost completely surrounded by water: the Mediterranean Sea, Atlantic Ocean, Red Sea and Indian Ocean. Just over half of Africa lies north of the Equator.

Africa is a continent of rich variety. It rarely rains in the Sahara Desert, where daytime temperatures occasionally exceed 50 °C. Not everywhere is dry and hot, however. The village of Debundscha, in Cameroon, is one of the wettest places on Earth, with more than 10 metres of rain falling on it each year. There are frozen glaciers on some mountains in East Africa, including Mount Kilimanjaro.

The vast Sahara Desert occupies much of the north of the continent.

GORILLA

GIRAFFE

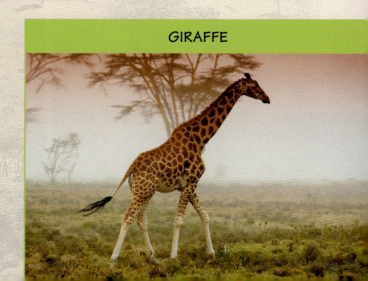

Two of the world's longest rivers are in Africa – the Nile (6,650 kilometres) and the Congo (4,700 kilometres).

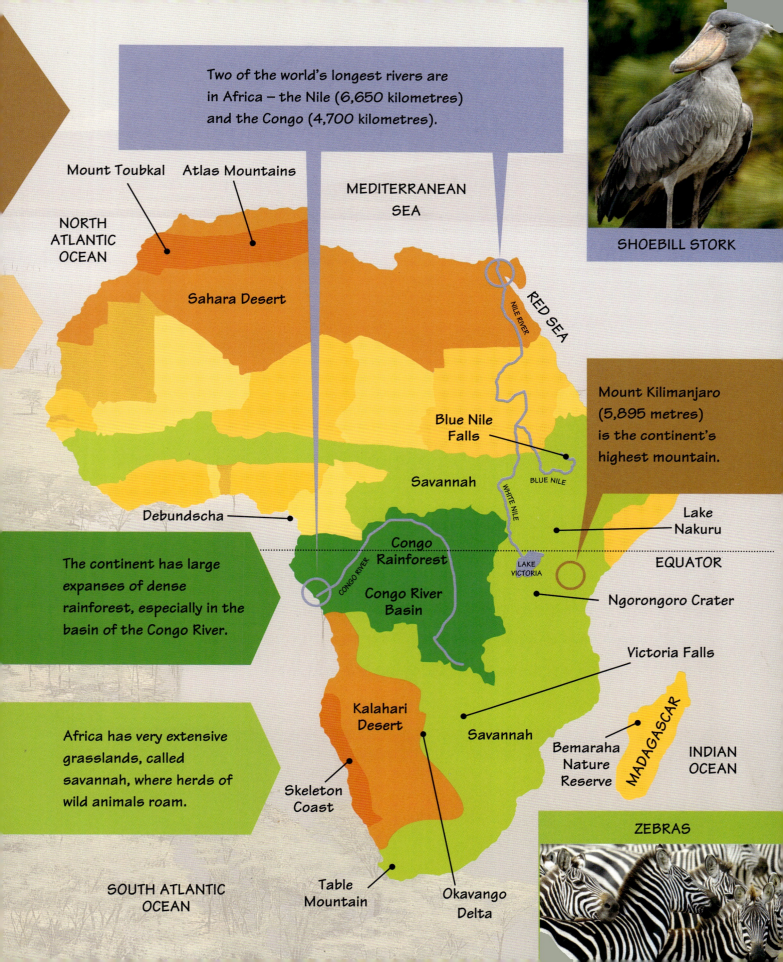

SHOEBILL STORK

Mount Toubkal   Atlas Mountains

MEDITERRANEAN SEA

NORTH ATLANTIC OCEAN

RED SEA

Sahara Desert

NILE RIVER

Mount Kilimanjaro (5,895 metres) is the continent's highest mountain.

Blue Nile Falls

Savannah

BLUE NILE

WHITE NILE

Debundscha

Lake Nakuru

The continent has large expanses of dense rainforest, especially in the basin of the Congo River.

Congo Rainforest

CONGO RIVER

Congo River Basin

LAKE VICTORIA

EQUATOR

Ngorongoro Crater

Victoria Falls

Africa has very extensive grasslands, called savannah, where herds of wild animals roam.

Kalahari Desert

Savannah

MADAGASCAR

Bemaraha Nature Reserve

INDIAN OCEAN

Skeleton Coast

ZEBRAS

SOUTH ATLANTIC OCEAN

Table Mountain

Okavango Delta

Table Mountain

Looming 1,086 metres high above the South African city of Cape Town, Table Mountain gets its name from its flat top and very steep sides. From the summit, there are amazing views over the Atlantic Ocean.

Table Mountain is made of hard sandstone rocks, millions of years old. The rocks were formed in an ancient valley and then lifted high by movements of the Earth's crust. A 'tablecloth' of cloud often rests on top of the mountain. It forms when moist onshore wind rises over it and cools. The moisture helps an amazing array of wildflowers to grow on the mountain.

Flowers bloom on Table Mountain all year, but the mix of colours varies according to the season. There may be pink-and-white proteas (left), mauve-and-yellow sorrels, and other red, orange, blue and white blooms.

Cape sugarbirds (right), butterflies and beetles visit flowers to feed on nectar.

TABLECLOTH

Table Mountain ghost frogs live in streams that flow down the mountain – and they live nowhere else on Earth.

Rock hyraxes scuttle up and down the steep slopes in search of plants to nibble.

Skeleton Coast

The sandy coastline that runs between the cold Atlantic Ocean and the dry Namib Desert in southern Africa is named the Skeleton Coast because of the numbers of whale and seal bones that once littered the shore. Today, the 'skeletons' of shipwrecks slowly decay here.

The coast separates two very different worlds. The waters offshore are teeming with life – fish, dolphins, seals and seabirds. Inland is a vast landscape of orange and red sand dunes. Some can reach 300 metres high. There are shrubs but no trees. The only animals here are those that can survive with very little fresh water. They include scorpions, snakes, lizards and antelopes.

Cape fur seals hunt fish in the sea. They come ashore to rest.

The cold waters of the Benguela Current flow north, close to the coast. The current cools the wind passing over it, and thick fog forms in the moist air. Many ships have lost their way in the fog and run aground.

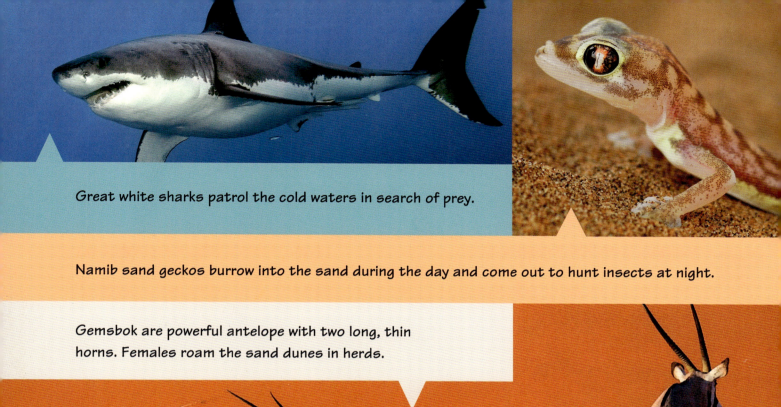

Great white sharks patrol the cold waters in search of prey.

Namib sand geckos burrow into the sand during the day and come out to hunt insects at night.

Gemsbok are powerful antelope with two long, thin horns. Females roam the sand dunes in herds.

Okavango Delta

The Okavango River flows from the highlands of Angola and into the Kalahari Desert – but it never reaches the ocean. Instead, it ends up in a flat, swampy area of southern Africa called the Okavango Delta.

From May to September, the river fills the delta with water. The water attracts thousands of animals. Buffalo, elephants, antelope and birds visit – along with the leopards, lions and hyenas that hunt them. Many of the animals come to breed and raise young. When the flood waters drain away, the animals move on.

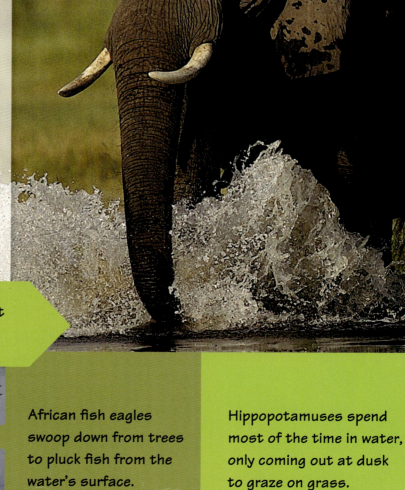

Large herds of African elephants visit the delta for its lush vegetation.

African fish eagles swoop down from trees to pluck fish from the water's surface.

Hippopotamuses spend most of the time in water, only coming out at dusk to graze on grass.

Part of the Okavango Delta is protected in the Moremi Game Reserve. People of the BaTawana tribe live in this area of woodland, marshes, grassland and lakes. Heavy rain and thunderstorms are frequent from December to February.

Dropwing dragonflies perch on reeds in marshy areas.

Victoria Falls

At the border between Zimbabwe and Zambia, the waters of the mighty Zambezi River thunder over a cliff and into a deep chasm. These are the Victoria Falls. The waterfall is the largest in the world, twice the height of the Niagara Falls in the USA.

Before it reaches the waterfall, the Zambezi flows over tough rock called basalt. The gorge into which it now crashes was a vertical band of soft sandstone rock. Over thousands of years, the force of the river has worn away the softer rock, creating a gorge 1,500 metres wide and more than 100 metres deep.

The force of the water plunging into the chasm can be heard a long way off, and it throws up a cloud of mist that can be seen many kilometres away. That is why the local Kalolo-Lozi people called it *Mosi-oa-tunya*, 'the smoke that thunders'.

Waterbuck live close to the Zambezi River; only the males have horns.

Close to the falls, blood lilies grow in the moist and shady forests.

13

Madagascar

Situated in the Indian Ocean off the east coast of Africa, Madagascar is the fourth largest island in the world. Many of its plants, and animals including lemurs, tenrecs and fossas, live here and nowhere else on Earth.

Madagascar's eastern side is covered by dense and lush tropical rainforests. For eight months of the year, the western side is bone-dry. The only plants that grow here are those that can survive the yearly drought. Baobab trees store water in their trunks, and acacias have very long tap roots to reach water far below the surface. When the rains arrive in December the countryside becomes greener.

Bemaraha Nature Reserve has an extraordinary landscape of savannah, undisturbed forest, and limestone 'needles', called tsingy (below). Fish eagles hunt in the reddish-brown waters of the Manambolo River, while lemurs (right) live in the forest.

Giant baobab trees can grow to heights of 30 metres.

The Malagasy giant chameleon lives in trees, where it preys on large insects.

The fossa is a cat-like carnivore that hunts by day and night.

Great Rift Valley

The Great Rift Valley runs for thousands of kilometres from the Red Sea in the north to the coast of Mozambique in the south. The valley has been forming for 35 million years along a line where Earth's crust is very slowly splitting apart. The very first humans are believed to have lived in the valley.

Along its length are dozens of volcanoes and many shallow, mineral-rich lakes, such as Nakuru and Bogoria. These are called soda lakes because they are very alkaline. Lake Nakuru is shallow enough for a person to wade across it; this is ideal for wading birds, such as the hundreds of thousands of long-legged, pink flamingos that live here.

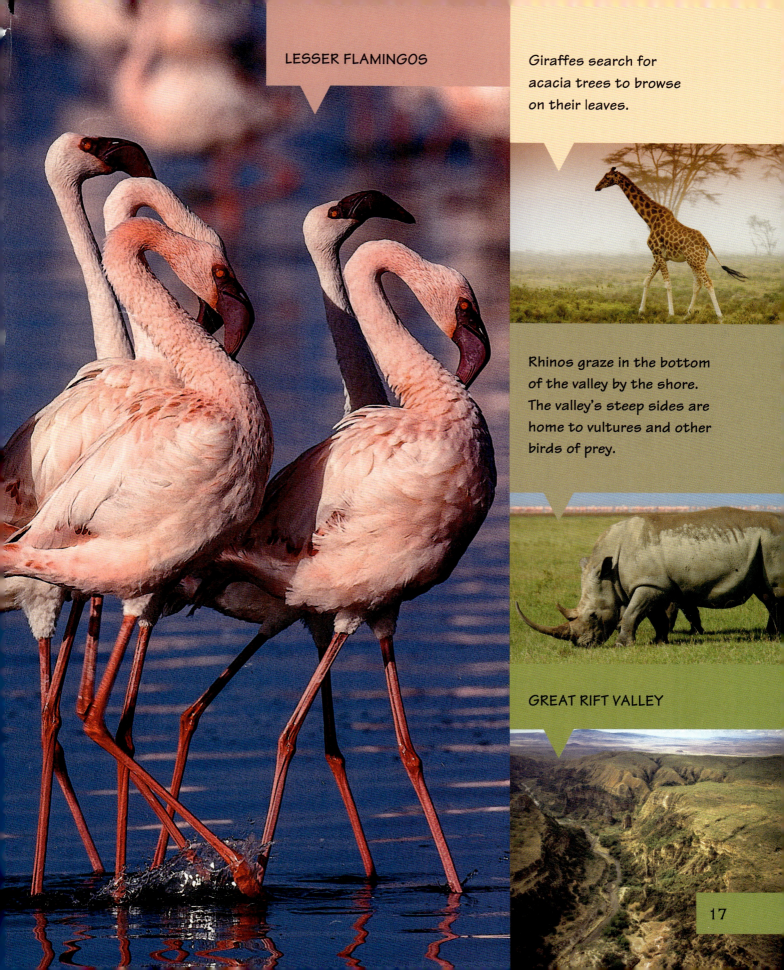

LESSER FLAMINGOS

Giraffes search for acacia trees to browse on their leaves.

Rhinos graze in the bottom of the valley by the shore. The valley's steep sides are home to vultures and other birds of prey.

GREAT RIFT VALLEY

17

Ngorongoro Crater

In the north-east of Tanzania's vast savannah lies the Ngorongoro Crater. It is all that remains of a huge volcano that exploded and collapsed more than two million years ago.

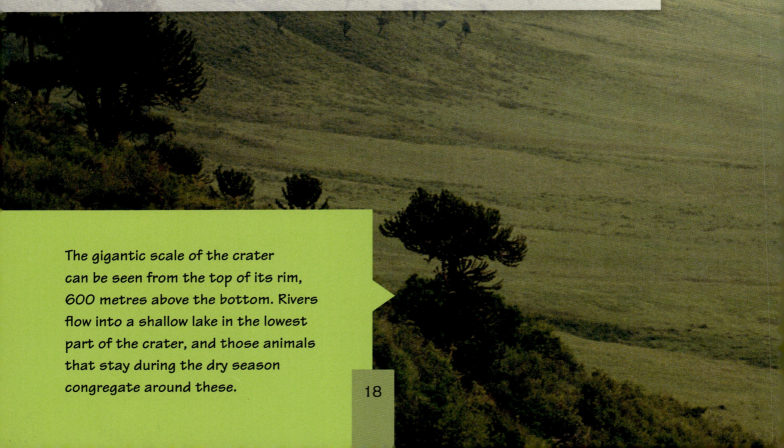

The inside of the crater is now an expanse of grassland that provides lush feeding for tens of thousands of animals. Buffalo, zebras, wildebeest, gazelles and elephants feed there. In May, early in the dry season, herds of wildebeest thousands strong leave the crater in search of fresh grazing and water. They are often accompanied by zebras and gazelles. The animals return at the start of the rainy season in November.

The gigantic scale of the crater can be seen from the top of its rim, 600 metres above the bottom. Rivers flow into a shallow lake in the lowest part of the crater, and those animals that stay during the dry season congregate around these.

These wildebeest and zebras are at the start of their annual migration north.

The Ngorongoro Crater has one of the highest concentrations of lions in East Africa.

Mount Kilimanjaro

Kilimanjaro is a dormant volcano that towers high over the plains of Tanzania and Kenya. At 5,895 metres above sea level, it is Africa's highest mountain. Despite being close to the Equator, its summit is bitterly cold, especially at night. It snows frequently, and there is always ice near the summit.

Few large animals live on the higher parts of the mountain, but lower down there is forest, where birds, colobus monkeys and African elephants live. Above the treeline and below the icy summit, there is moorland and cold desert. In recent years, thousands of trees have been planted on the lower slopes to reduce soil erosion.

The conical shape of Kilimanjaro is typical of a volcano. One of its three volcanic cones is called Kibo. It has openings, called fumaroles, which emit hot gases from deep underground. Kibo hasn't erupted for thousands of years, but it could do one day.

Black and white colobus monkeys have spectacularly long tails; they live in forests on the lower slopes.

While feeding on nectar, sunbirds pollinate flowers, such as lobelias (below).

Giant lobelias are slow-growing but long-lived plants of Kilimanjaro's upper slopes.

Congo Rainforest

Within the basin of the Congo River, in Central Africa, is the second-largest rainforest on Earth. At two million square kilometres, it is larger than Germany, France and Spain combined. Only the Amazon Rainforest in South America is larger.

The Congo Rainforest is home to more than 11,000 different kinds of plants. Some of the forest is so dense that it has probably never been explored by people. Scientists think that many thousands of beetles and bugs live in the depths of the forest that no one has ever seen. The rainforest is drained by massive rivers, including the Congo itself, and the Lomami and Ubangi rivers. People have cleared parts of the forest for its wood, or to make space for agriculture and towns.

OKAPI

Some areas, such as Virunga National Park, are protected for their fascinating animals and plants. These areas are a refuge for rare forest elephants, gorillas, okapis and bonobos (pygmy chimpanzees).

Despite their fearsome appearance, mountain gorillas eat mostly fruit and leaves, with a few termites and caterpillars.

White-crested hornbills are large birds, but they are usually seen only when they fly from one tree to another.

African giant swallowtails are the largest butterflies in the world, with a wingspan of 23 centimetres.

Nile River

From the north end of Lake Victoria in Uganda to the coast of Egypt, where its waters enter the Mediterranean Sea, the Nile River flows 6,650 kilometres through mountains, deserts, lush oases and marshes. It is the world's longest river.

The Nile is a lifeline. It provides water to drink and to irrigate crops, fish to eat, and is an important transportation route. People have sailed wooden boats called feluccas on the Nile for thousands of years. About 5,000 years ago, the ancient Egyptian civilization began to develop alongside the river. Pyramids and temples from that era can still be seen today.

The impressive Blue Nile Falls (above) are close to the source of the Blue Nile, in the Ethiopian Highlands. From there, the river descends rapidly to meet the other branch of the river, the White Nile, at Khartoum. It then crosses a huge, marshy plain before crashing down a series of rapids and finally meandering at a much more leisurely pace through Egypt.

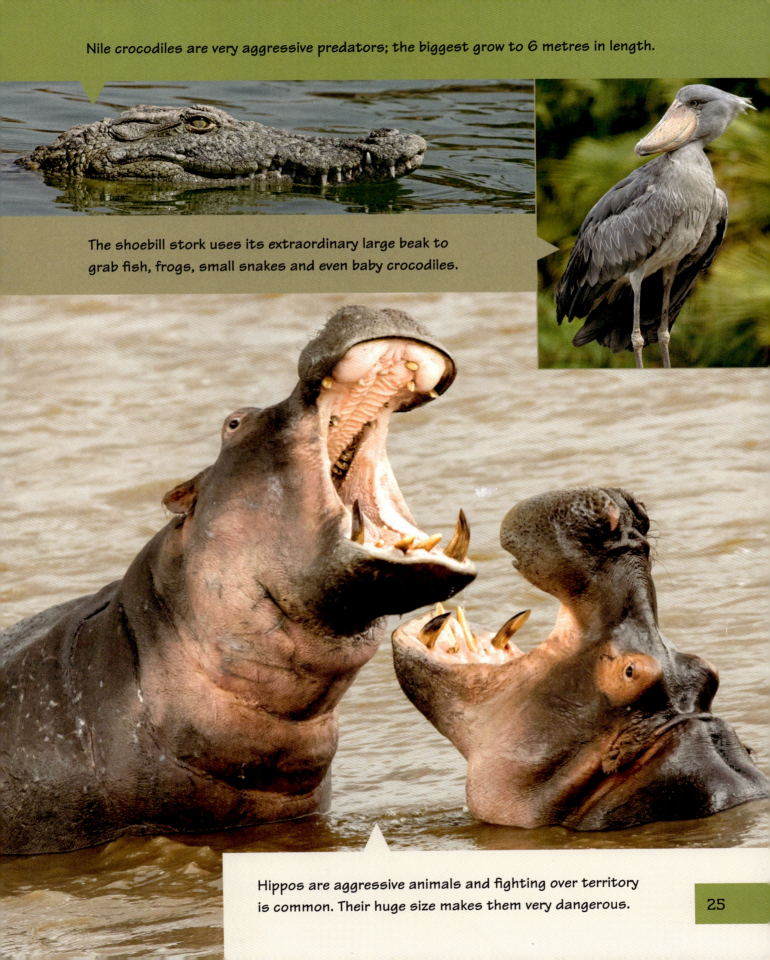

Nile crocodiles are very aggressive predators; the biggest grow to 6 metres in length.

The shoebill stork uses its extraordinary large beak to grab fish, frogs, small snakes and even baby crocodiles.

Hippos are aggressive animals and fighting over territory is common. Their huge size makes them very dangerous.

Sahara Desert

Stretching from the Red Sea in the east to the Atlantic Ocean, the vast Sahara is the world's biggest desert. It is bigger than the USA. Some areas are covered by fields of sand dunes that are constantly being moved by the wind. Other regions are stony or rocky.

The Sahara is a difficult place for animals to survive. It is baking hot by day, and sometimes cold at night. There is little water and often no plant life. Yet lots of animals do live here. By day, most keep out of the scorching sunshine by hiding in crevices between rocks or burying themselves in the sand. They come out at night, when it is cooler, to feed and hunt.

All dromedary camels are domesticated animals. For thousands of years desert people have used camels to carry loads.

The Sahara sand viper is a venomous snake that buries itself in the sand so it can ambush prey – and stay cool!

In the mountains of Tassili du Hoggar, in the central Sahara, there are sandstone peaks that have been shaped by the wind. For thousands of years, the Tuareg people have lived in this area, which has green oases and 6,000-year-old rock paintings.

In northern Algeria, the Western Sand Sea, or erg, is one of the most barren places on Earth. There are no permanent villages, no roads crossing it and no vegetation. Everything is covered with enormous sand dunes.

When too hot, the fennec fox loses heat through its remarkably large ears. It usually hunts at night.

Atlas Mountains

In the far north of Africa, lying between the Mediterranean Sea and the Sahara Desert, the Atlas Mountains are rich in natural resources. Trees for timber are grown on the forested lower slopes, and copper, salt and even silver are buried underground.

There are many mountain ridges, covered with forests of oak, cedar and fir trees. The ridges are separated by valleys and steep-sided gorges, through which rivers tumble over waterfalls and rapids. Climbing even higher, the forests thin out and are replaced with meadows, which are warm in summer but very cold in winter. In spring and summer, the meadows are alive with wildflowers and butterflies.

Mount Toubkal is the highest peak in the Atlas Mountains, rising more than 4,000 metres above sea level. Many trekkers make the long climb to its rocky summit in spring and summer. In winter, the higher slopes are covered with snow.

A great variety of butterflies are found here, which includes the Spanish festoon (left), Moroccan marbled white and common tiger blue.

Barbary macaques live in groups called troops in forested parts of the Atlas Mountains.

29

Glossary

alkaline containing salts that neutralise acids

ambush a surprise attack

barren land with little or no vegetation

bask lie in the sun

browse feed on leaves and twigs that are high up

chasm a deep, steep-sided cleft in the ground

congregate form a crowd

conical shaped like a cone

crater bowl-shaped depression around a volcano, or where a volcano once was

crust the outermost layer of planet Earth

current water that is moving in one direction

delta the area where a river drops its sediment as it enters a lake or the ocean

desert a place that receives little or no rainfall and has few plants or none at all

domesticated tame farm or pet animals

dormant not active, temporarily

dry season the part of the year when very little rain falls

Equator an imaginary line around Earth that is an equal distance from the North and South Poles

irrigate to add water to land artificially

meandering winding first one way, then the other

migrate move from one region to another according to the seasons

mineral a natural substance, such as salt, which is made of chemicals and usually forms in the shape of a crystal

moorland an open hilly area with low-lying vegetation

oases fertile areas with water in a desert

pollinate transfer pollen from one flower to

another, so fertilising the second flower

rainy season the part of the year when most of the rain falls

rapids a fast-flowing and turbulent part of a river

sandstone sedimentary rock made of sand or quartz grains that have been compressed together

sediment mud and sand carried by rivers and streams

source place where a river starts

summit the very top

tap roots roots that grow vertically downwards

tenrec a small insect-eating mammal that looks like a small hedgehog or otter

venomous producing chemicals that can injure or kill prey

Books

Animal Families (series) by Tim Harris (Wayland, 2014)
Close-up Continents: Mapping Africa by Paul Rockett (Franklin Watts, 2016)
Expedition Diaries: African Savannah by Simon Chapman (Franklin Watts, 2018)
Travelling Wild: Journey Along the River Nile by Sonya Newland (Wayland, 2016)
Travelling Wild: Trekking in the Congo Rainforest by Alex Woolf (Wayland, 2014)

Websites

Facts for Kids
This website has lots of interesting and fun facts on the African continent.
www.kids-world-travel-guide.com/africa-facts.html

Geography for Kids
Discover profiles of every country in Africa.
www.ducksters.com/geography/africa.php

Go Wild
Learn more about your favourite animals in these WWF fact files.
gowild.wwf.org.uk/regions/africa-fact-files

National Geographic Animal Pictures and Facts
Simply type in the animals you're interested in and get lots of fascinating facts. The site covers mammals, reptiles, amphibians, fish and birds.
www.nationalgeographic.com/animals/index/

National Geographic Kids [resources for educators]
The search tool enables access to a great range of resources, from a classroom safari in Namibia to a chimp rescue mission.
www.natgeokids.com/uk/teacher-category/animals/

Note to parents and teachers: Every effort has been made by the Publishers to ensure that the websites in this book are of the highest educational value, and that they contain no inappropriate or offensive material. However, because of the nature of the Internet, it is impossible to guarantee that the contents of these sites will not be altered. We strongly advise that Internet access is supervised by a responsible adult.

Further information

Index